4-7

WOODS BRANCH
GROSSE POINTE PUBLIC LIBRARY
GROSSE POINTE, MI 48236
MAR 1 1 2009

The SPECTACULAR TRUE STORY of Annette Kellerman, WHO SWAM HER WAY TO Fame, Fortune & Swimsuit History!

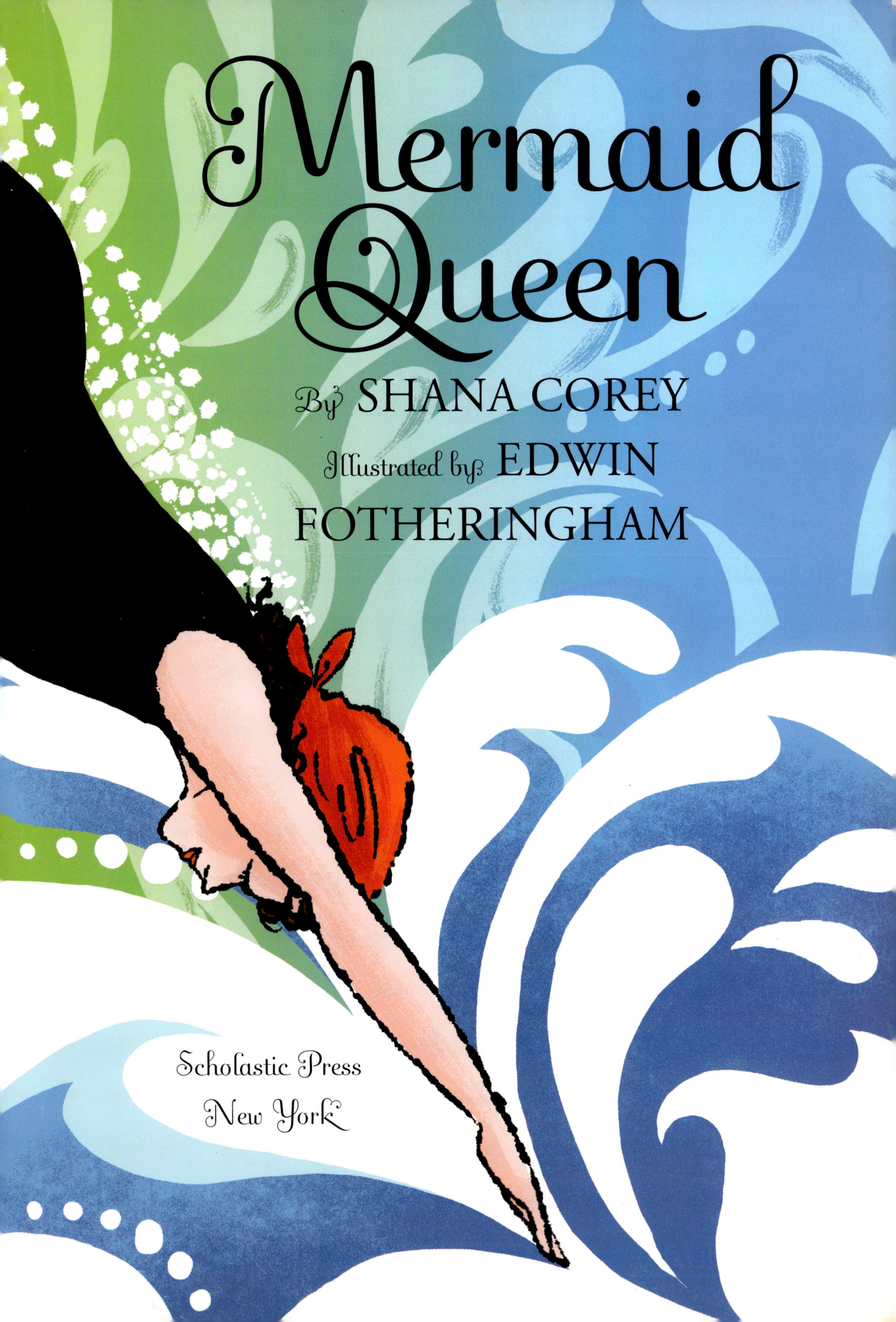

Text copyright © 2009 by Shana Corey
Illustrations copyright © 2009 by Edwin Fotheringham
All rights reserved. Published by Scholastic Press, an Imprint of Scholastic Inc., *Publishers since 1920.*
SCHOLASTIC, SCHOLASTIC PRESS, and associated logos are trademarks and/or registered trademarks of Scholastic Inc.

No part of this publication may be reproduced, stored in a retrieval system, or transmitted in any form or by any means,
electronic, mechanical, photocopying, recording, or otherwise, without written permission of the publisher.
For information regarding permission, write to Scholastic Inc.,
Attention: Permissions Department, 557 Broadway, New York, NY 10012.

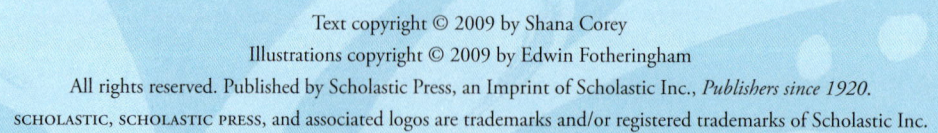

Corey, Shana.
Mermaid Queen: the spectacular true story of Annette Kellerman, who swam her way to fame,
fortune, & swimsuit history! / by Shana Corey; illustrated by Edwin Fotheringham. p. cm.
ISBN-13: 978-0-439-69835-1
ISBN-10: 0-439-69835-9
1. Kellerman, Annette, 1888-1975. 2. Swimmers—Australia—Biography—Juvenile literature.
3. Women swimmers—Australia—Biography—Juvenile literature. I. Fotheringham, Edwin. II. Title.
GV838.K45C67 2008 797.2'1092—dc22 [B] 2007052664

10 9 8 7 6 5 4 3 2 1   09 10 11 12 13

Printed in Singapore   46
First edition, February 2009

The text type was set in Adobe Garamond Pro. The display type was set in Fling.
Illustrations were done in digital media. Book design by Marijka Kostiw

For Jack and Nathan,
with all my love. —S.C.

For my wife, Becky,
and my kids, Anna and Joe.
I'm a lucky guy. —E.F.

When Annette was a little girl, she lived in a house by the sea in Australia.

Annette's parents were music teachers and her house was filled with singing and dancing and music. Every day Annette watched the dancers twirl and dip and whirl. She dreamt that one day she would be one of them—beautiful and graceful and fancy-free.

But Annette couldn't dance.

She could hardly even walk.

To strengthen her legs, Annette's father taught her to swim. Annette swam and swam, and the more she swam, the stronger she grew.

Pretty soon she was slicing through the water—winning races and setting records.

But in 1903, people weren't used to seeing female athletes. Annette's mother worried that people would talk. She wished Annette would do something more artistic.

But swimming had made Annette's legs **strong**. And in the water, she didn't feel plain or clumsy or weak. She felt beautiful and graceful and 𝓯𝓪𝓷𝓬𝔂-𝓯𝓻𝓮𝓮.

Annette kept practicing her strokes and making waves. When she wasn't racing, she daydreamed about the ballerinas she'd loved as a little girl. She whirled and twirled. She 𝓭𝓲𝓹𝓹𝓮𝓭 and 𝓭𝓪𝓷𝓬𝓮𝓭 and 𝓭𝓲𝓿𝓮𝓭.

No one was sure exactly what it was she was doing, but Annette didn't care one bit. She 𝓵𝓸𝓿𝓮𝓭 her new invention. It wasn't quite ballet, and it wasn't quite swimming —it was water 𝓫𝓪𝓵𝓵𝓮𝓽!

Swimming and diving filled Annette with *joy*.

She wanted to show other girls how **wonderful** they could be.

She demonstrated her *dazzling* dives at the local aquarium.

"A fine performance!" trumpeted the papers.

Annette and her father decided to show the world Annette's invention

and *exactly* what girls could do in the water.

They said good-bye to Australia

and sailed for England.

When they arrived in London, they went to Soho and the Strand, Picadilly and the Palace, hoping to put on a show. But everywhere they went, people just scoffed.

A girl swimmer?

Too plain. Too plump. Too weird. Too wet. Too bad!

Annette remembered her mother's worries. If people saw a girl swimmer, they might talk. But maybe that was just what she needed! Maybe Annette should do something drastic to get people talking about girl athletes!

Annette and her father rowed out to the middle of the yucky, mucky River Thames. She dove into the murky water. She swam for thirteen miles up the river, dodging tugs and barges the whole way.

"Lumme. You're a girl!" gasped the watchman when he pulled her out.

Now people were paying attention!

A newspaper even asked if Annette would try to swim the English Channel. The English Channel separated France and England. It was twenty-two miles wide! Only one man—and no woman—had ever made it across.

Annette and her father traveled to Dover to train.

For the next six weeks, she swam from one seaside resort to another.

When the big day arrived, Annette dove off a pier into the cold water.

Splash!

She swam toward France, accompanied by a steam tug and a rowboat. Whenever she got hungry, she slurped chicken soup or hot chocolate through a long-snouted cup or snacked on tiny sandwiches held out on the end of a long stick.

Annette had outdistanced the other swimmers by a mile, when she got seasick.

She didn't make it to France. But people marveled over the young girl who had swum so far and so well.

Why, she even made it look artistic!

Now all of England was talking about the

Mermaid Queen from Australia.

It wasn't long before Annette received an invitation to perform before royalty at London's Bath Club. Annette knew her mother would be proud.

But just as she was about to go on, the stage manager rushed over. He told her she couldn't *possibly* show her bare legs.

Annette had come so far—she couldn't let something as silly as a swimsuit get in her way!

She

thought

fast . . .

After the performance at the Bath Club, word of the star swimmer spread farther.

Soon Annette was racing her way through Europe.

Vienna

Hurra! Wunderbar!

Next, Annette was invited to America to swim at Wonderland Park in Boston's Revere Beach. *America*—the land of *free*! Annette couldn't wait.

But when she arrived at Revere Beach, she was amazed at what the American ladies were wearing: stockings and shoes, bloomers and bathing dresses, collars and corsets and caps—all for a day at the beach! While the men and boys splashed in the surf, the waterlogged ladies could only bob up and down near the shore. *How could anyone possibly swim in that?*

"My word!" marveled Annette. Then she slipped on her racing suit and dove into the water.

Splash!

The Bostonians were beside themselves!

They screeched and squealed and shrieked with terror.

"Hey—what are you doing in that suit?" asked a policeman.

Annette was arrested!

"Your Honor," Annette told the judge.
"Swimming is the most wonderful and healthy exercise. Why, every child in America should be taught to swim."
The crowd gasped.
Then Annette asked the judge how women could *possibly* be expected to swim in bathing suits that felt like lead chains?!
Everyone waited to see what would happen.

Would Annette be banned from Boston? Would the judge send her to jail?

No!

The judge let Annette go.

The next morning, the beach was filled with reporters waiting to see what kind of waves Annette would make now.

At the water's edge, she threw off her robe.

Flash went the cameras.

"Ooh," breathed the crowds.

Annette dove into the cool blue water.

She whirled and twirled. She dipped and dived.

From the shore, the ladies watched in their hot, heavy suits.

Eventually, some of them tried Annette's style. They swam out

in the surf in their sleek new suits.

They whirled and twirled and dipped and dived.

"Aahhh,"

they sighed with relief.

Author's Note

I have always been interested in women and girls brave enough to make waves. So when I first saw a passing reference to Annette Kellerman, champion swimmer, risk-tasker, and fashion rebel who invented both water ballet *and* the modern swimsuit, I had to know more.

Few people have heard of Annette today, but in her time she was a household name. At the peak of her fame, she was not only a renowned athlete but a bestselling author, an outspoken advocate for women's health and dress reform, and a celebrated stage and movie star who grabbed headlines whatever she did and earned the nickname the "Mermaid Queen."

What drew me most to Annette, though, wasn't that she succeeded at so many things—but that she *didn't* always succeed. Still, she was brave and determined enough to keep trying, even when the rest of the world was telling her not to. To me, that sort of conviction—the courage to believe in yourself even when others doubt you—is one of the most difficult and bravest things of all.

THE NEW WOMAN

Annette Kellerman was born on July 6, 1886, in Sydney, Australia. As a child, a medical condition (possibly rickets) forced her to wear heavy leg braces. A doctor suggested she learn to swim to strengthen her legs. Annette remembered being "terribly afraid of the water" and later said that it took her much longer to learn to swim than her siblings. Nevertheless, she persevered and was soon setting records.

Annette began her swimming career at a time of great change for female athletes. The "New Woman" was coming into vogue—a woman who was not the protected flower that had been held up as the ideal for her grandmother's generation, but who was educated and enthusiastic, who valued her independence and might perhaps have a job outside the home, who preferred comfortable clothes to corsets, and who was athletic and might ride a bicycle or enjoy archery.

However, even during this time of change, professional female athletes were not held in high regard. The first modern Olympic Games, which took place in Athens in 1896, didn't include women; and while some scientists were beginning to recognize the health benefits of exercise, many worried that too much exercise might be harmful to women's "fragile nerves" and their ability to have children.

Things were a little freer in Australia, but Annette still had to overcome obstacles at home. Her mother was opposed to her becoming a professional athlete and wanted her to have a career in the arts. Annette thought swimming could be an artistic achievement in itself, and was determined to prove that to the world.

"A MILLSTONE AROUND ONE'S NECK"

Annette believed swimming was "the best sport in the world for women" and was passionate about its benefits. "An occasional swim does as much good as a six months' vacation," she promised in her book *How to Swim* (1918).

She was just as passionate in her condemnation of the proper but cumbersome ladies' bathing costumes of the time, comparing them to a "Biblical millstone around one's neck" and arguing, "there is no more reason why you should wear . . . those awkward, unnecessary, lumpy 'bathing suits,' than there is that you should wear lead chains."

Annette herself had always worn a boy's racing suit for her distance swims. The suit was accepted for racing (female events were often segregated and racers usually wore cloaks over their suits until the moment they dived in), but it created a stir when Annette tried to perform in it at London's exclusive Bath Club (she appeased the club by sewing stockings onto the suit).

New England wasn't quite ready for the short suit either. And it caused a scandal when Annette wore it for a distance swim in Boston Harbor in the summer of 1908. Annette made amends again by introducing a new suit, slightly altered from the boys' racing suit with a nod to a more feminine style. The new suit had a "knit stockingette" that formed a short, close-fitting skirt over the suit. According to Annette, the first time she wore it "the ohs and the ahs were all, this time, in admiration. Women rushed up asking where they could buy such a suit."

Annette posing in a version of the suit she created at London's Bath Club

Annette's suit soon became the norm, and the subsequent publicity led to worldwide fame for Annette and eventually helped bring about a more relaxed attitude toward women's swimwear.

"QUEEN OF THE MERMAIDS"

While Annette was in Boston, a Harvard professor wrote an article naming her the perfect woman. Never a traditional beauty, Annette attributed the title to her physical fitness and quipped, "I'm the perfect woman from the neck down." Now a role model, Annette became a respected advocate for health and fitness. President Roosevelt once even summoned her to talk to him about her water cure.

Annette was dismayed that girls were taught "it is most unlady-like to be possessed of legs or to know how to use them." She believed exercise was key not just to health but to self-esteem. "The enjoyment of splashing about cannot compare with the greater joy that comes with a feeling that you can take care of yourself in the water," she wrote in *Ladies' Home Journal* in 1910.

Annette went on to pioneer and star in the first silent-movie water spectaculars, among them *Neptune's Daughter* (1914) and *Daughter of the Gods* (1916). In 1917, her lifelong dream of stage success was fulfilled when she starred at New York City's Hippodrome Theater as the Queen of the Mermaids. With this perfomance Annette felt she'd finally lived up to her mother's artistic ambitions for her.

Annette wrote two bestsellers on fitness, *How to Swim* and *Physical Beauty: How to Keep It* (1918), which offer sound advice even today—encouraging people to eat wheat bread instead of white, to eat more salad and drink lots of water, and to avoid alcohol and caffeine. She later ran a health food store, and at age seventy-five told a reporter that she still swam every day (and claimed that she usually followed her swims with a few push-ups and cartwheels!).

In 1952, a film was made of her life, *The Million Dollar Mermaid* starring Esther Williams. "That film of my life wasn't half as exciting as it's really been," noted Annette.

Swimming never lost its magic for her. "I learn much from people in the way they meet the unknown of life, and water is a great test. . . . This love of the unknown is the greatest of all the joys which swimming has for me."

After a long, successful career, Annette said that her greatest achievements were freeing women from their oppressive bathing suits, and the knowledge that her "work has stimulated an interest in swimming as a woman's sport." Upon her death on November 6, 1975, her ashes were scattered near the Great Barrier Reef in Australia.

Acknowledgments

This story wouldn't have been possible without the help of a great many people who generously shared their knowledge with me. In alphabetical order they are: Kevin John Berry; Elizabeth Bouvier of the Massachusetts Police Archives; Ian Collie, producer of the documentary *The Original Mermaid*; Ned Comstock, Curator for Performing Arts at the USC Cinema-Television Library; Barbara Firth, co-author of *The Original Million Dollar Mermaid*; Sean Fisher of the Metropolitan District Commission Archives in Boston; Mark Frost of the Dover Museum in Dover, England; Peter McCauley, Revere Beach Historian; Diane Shepard of the Lynn Museum; and Dr. Brian Wimborne.

Special thanks to Emily Gibson, biographer, co-author (along with with Barbara Firth) of *The Original Million Dollar Mermaid* (Allen and Unwyn, 2005), for her time and expertise in reviewing this book.

And always and especially, thank you to everyone at Scholastic Press, in particular Abby Ranger; Marijka Kostiw, incredibly talented art director; and my very smart, very kind, *very* patient, editor, Tracy Mack, who not only made this book possible but made it better at every turn.

Of many sources consulted, the following were particularly helpful. *The Bulletin* (April 26, 1902, and May 2, 1903); *The London Times* (June 20, July 27, August 8, August 25, and September 11, 1905); *The New York Times* (November 19, 1916; October 9, 1953); *The Boston Evening Transcript* (July 30 and 31, 1908); *The Revere Journal* (June 13, July 25, and August 1 and 29, 1908); *Ladies' Home Journal* (August 1910 and July 1915); *American Magazine* (March 1917); *People* (Sydney, May 23, 1951); *The Boston Sunday Globe* (October 11, 1953); *Melbourne Herald* (October 30, 1956); *The Courier-Mail* (November 7, 1975); and *Winning Ways: A Photo History of American Women in Sports* by Sue Macy (Scholastic, 1996). I am also extremely indebted to Annette Kellerman's *How to Swim* and *Physical Beauty and How to Keep It* (George Doran Company, NY, 1918), and to *My Story*, Annette Kellerman's unpublished autobiographical script treatment for the movie *The Million Dollar Mermaid*, kindly shared with me by The USC Cinema-Television Library.

Quotes were drawn from the following:
p. 17 "A fine performance!" (*The Bulletin*, May 2, 1903, p. 14)
p. 20 "Lumme, you're a girl!" (*People*, Sydney, May 23, 1951)
p. 32 "My word!" (*My Story*, p. 39)
p. 32 "Hey—what are you doing in that suit?" (*My Story*, p. 39)
p. 34 "Your Honor, swimming is the most wonderful . . ." (*My Story*, p. 40)
p. 42 "Terribly afraid . . ." (*American Magazine*, March 1917)
p. 43 "Best sport in the world . . ." (*How to Swim*, p. 38)
p. 43 "An occasional swim . . ." (*How to Swim*, p. 53)
p. 43 "Biblical millstone . . . lead chains" (*How to Swim*, p. 47)
p. 43 "the ohs and ahs . . ." (*My Story*, p. 41)
p. 44 "I'm the perfect woman . . ." (*People*, Sydney, May 23, 1951)
p. 44 "It is most unlady-like to be possessed of legs . . ." (*How to Swim*, p. 45)
p. 44 "The enjoyment . . ." (*Ladies' Home Journal*, August 1910)
p. 44 "That film of my life . . ." (*Melbourne Herald*, October 30, 1956, p. 11)
p. 44 "I learn much from people . . ." (*How to Swim*, p. 37)
p. 44 "Work has stimulated an interest in swimming . . ." (*Physical Beauty*, p. 85)